OBJECTS AND FURNITURE DESIGN

CHARLES AND RAY EAMES

Photographic credits

Eames Office (pp. 4-5, 8, 12, 25-28, 30-35, 37-38, 40, 42, 44, 46-48, 51-52, 54, 55, 60-62, 65, 68-69, 73, 78, 80-82, 86-87, 90-91, 94-95, 98-99, 103, 106, 110, 112-115, 117); Eames Office, courtesy of Bonhams (pp. 79, 93); Eames Office, courtesy of Vitra (pp. 19, 63); Roger Foley (pp. 29, 103); Herman Miller Inc. (pp. 39, 77, 96); Andrew Neuhart (pp. 36, 41, 72, 97, 104); Marvin Rand (p. 107); The Museum of Modern Art, New York (pp. 20, 22-23); Julius Shulman (pp. 74-75, 101); Vitra Design Museum (pp. 22, 89); James Wojcik (pp. 17)

The publishers have made every effort to trace the copyright holders of the photographs reproduced in this book. However, they would be pleased, if informed, to correct any errors or omissions in subsequent editions of this publication.

Researching and texts: Sandra Dachs, Patricia de Muga and Laura García Hintze
Design: mot_studio

ISBN: 978-84-343-1495-5

Available in USA and Canada through D.A.P./Distributed Art Publishers
155 Sixth Avenue, 2nd Floor, New York, N.Y. 10013
Tel. (212) 627-1999 Fax: (212) 627-9484

Excerpt of a statement of Charles Eames published in the catalogue of What is design? exhibition, Paris, Centre Georges Pompidou, 1969, p. 345.

OBJECTS AND FURNITURE DESIGN

CHARLES AND RAY EAMES

Introduction by Mathias Remmele

Edited by Sandra Dachs, Patricia de Muga
and Laura García Hintze

Ediciones Polígrafa

LIST OF CONTENTS

INTRODUCTION

MATHIAS REMMELE

The work of Charles and Ray Eames was once referred to by Rolf Fehlbaum, head of the renowned furniture company Vitra and one of the world's most knowledgeable people on the subject, as a 'continent'. This metaphor aptly illustrates the enormous influence of the Eameses on twentieth-century design and also alludes to the great depth and unparalleled diversity of their oeuvre. Learning about the body of work that Charles and Ray Eames developed over a period of almost four decades is in fact comparable to the exploration of a vast continent full of wonders and discoveries. This publication offers the opportunity to become familiar with what is today regarded as the most significant and exciting part of the Eames Continent: furniture design.

The Eames oeuvre is best understood as the product of a highly fruitful collaboration between two different personalities whose skills and talents were ideally complementary. Charles and Ray first met in 1940 at the Cranbrook Academy of Art near Detroit, Michigan. Under the Finnish architect Eliel Saarinen, one of its founders, Cranbrook had developed into a leading centre of American design. Charles Eames, who was born in 1907 in St. Louis, Missouri, was primarily active as an architect before becoming an instructor at the academy. Ray Eames was born as Bernice Alexandra Kaiser in 1912 in Sacramento, California. After studying art under the German painter Hans Hofmann in New York City and Provincetown during the 1930s, she enrolled at Cranbrook to round off her artistic training. The couple was married in 1941, moved to Los Angeles and established an office together. The early years of their collaborative work were largely devoted to the creation of many groundbreaking furniture designs, which established the international reputation of the Eames Office. It was augmented in the following decades by many innovative and highly publicised designs in other areas, including significant works of architecture (particularly the house they built for themselves in 1949), exhibitions, films, toys, graphics, textile designs and an immense number of photographs. The

Eameses' wide-ranging creative work, which has strongly influenced our understanding of design and the role of the designer in modern society, ended with Charles' death in 1978. Ray died ten years later. Yet core aspects of the Eameses' oeuvre, which embodies their humanist perspectives and visions, have remained permanently relevant and vital.

Among the many fields in which the Eameses were active during the course of their joint career, furniture design occupies a special place. Their earliest projects were related to the production of furniture, which brought both commercial and critical success. In this area they were able to merge Charles' architectural background and structural approach with Ray's artistic training and sure sense of colour, line and shape, thereby combining their individual strengths in an ideal and fruitful way. The development of an Eames design was a process of trial and error. It always included an exhaustive examination of a particular material, in order to determine whether it was suited not only to the functional purpose of the object, but also to industrial production techniques. Instead of relying on sketches and drawings, the Eameses constructed full-scale prototypes in their workshop, which allowed them to explore different aspects of a design's construction, aesthetic appearance and production. In a process that was often long and tedious, characterised by failures as well as breakthroughs, they acquired the necessary skills and knowledge for developing fundamental solutions to design problems. The lasting viability of Eames designs is based on structural integrity paired with meticulous detailing, a design philosophy that rejects coincidental or arbitrary solutions, and thinking based on the criteria of mass production.

The legendary competition 'Organic Design in Home Furnishings', organised in 1940 by the New York Museum of Modern Art, marked the Eameses' entry into the field of furniture design. Charles Eames collaborated with his friend and colleague Eero Saarinen on the project. Awarded first prize in the category of seating furniture, their Organic Chair still stands out among the competition designs. The jury—which included Marcel Breuer and Alvar Aalto—cited the technical innovation represented by this piece of furniture in addition to its aesthetic qualities: It was the first example of a moulded plywood chair shell with compound curves. This development was motivated by the desire to create a one-piece seat shell that would be comfortable without requiring extensive padding. Although the planned production of the Organic Chair was not achieved in the 1940s due to technological limitations and the scarcity of materials during World War II, its shape and construction is reflected in a number of subsequent Eames designs, and also in later chairs by Eero Saarinen.

During the Second World War, Charles and Ray Eames continued to work intensively with moulded plywood. In pursuit of a viable technique for moulding layered wood into three-dimensional shapes, they constructed an experimental curing oven in their own apartment during the early 1940s. They used this apparatus to apply pressure and heat to thin layers of resin-soaked wood, thereby bending the wooden plies into rigid shells with compound curves. Fully functional despite its provisional appearance, the so-called 'Kazam! machine' has earned a place in design history. Their first successful pieces were leg splints used to stabilise injured soldiers during transport, which were ordered in large numbers by the US Navy. Soon after the end of the war, the Eameses were able to utilise this know-how for civilian applications. In a short time, they created designs for chairs, tables, children's furniture, toys and partition screens, some of which were made exclusively

out of plywood, others of which combined plywood with tubular steel.

The Eames plywood chairs also introduced another important innovation: so-called 'shock mounts' were first used here to connect the wooden seat shells to the chair bases. These rubber buttons made it unnecessary to bore holes in the thin plywood shells, and also increased the chairs' structural flexibility and comfort.

Today's methods for moulding plywood into three-dimensional shapes are still largely the same as those developed by the Eameses more than fifty years ago. Their plywood furniture is characterised by comfort, lightness, efficient use of materials and structural logic. The elegant lines and flowing sculptural planes of the plywood shells give these chairs an unmistakable identity. At the same time, they embody the optimistic mood of the era in which they were conceived.

'Getting the most of the best to the greatest number of people for the least': With these words, Charles and Ray Eames described one of their main goals as furniture designers. Of all their designs, the Plastic Chairs come closest to achieving this ideal. For years the Eameses devoted themselves to the concept of developing a one-piece seat shell whose shape would fit the human body. After experiments with plywood and aluminium sheeting yielded unsatisfactory results, an alternative material caught their attention: fibreglass-reinforced polyester resin. This new plastic, which was still completely unknown in the field of furniture, made it possible to adapt the shell design to industrial production methods. The Eameses immediately recognised and utilised the advantages of the material: pleasant tactile qualities, malleability, static strength combined with a high degree of flexibility, and the fact that it was inexpensive and suitable for mass production.

The full plastic shell with armrests (armchair shell) appeared on the market in 1950, quickly followed by the dining chair (side shell), as the first mass-produced plastic chairs in the history of furniture. The Eameses subsequently developed a variety of different bases for the shells, thereby expanding the potential applications of the plastic chairs. They were used in homes, in public offices and practices, and also for mass seating in restaurants, schools, auditoriums, airports and athletic stadiums.

A keen interest in industrial materials and innovative production methods, along with a preference for lightweight, but robust structures, were essential aspects of Charles and Ray Eames' design approach. Against this backdrop, it is hardly surprising that they experimented extensively with wire mesh—although this material (like fibreglass) had previously played a negligible role in the furniture industry. The Eameses first gained familiarity with wire mesh in 1950, when they developed new bases for their plastic chair shells and a low occasional table.

By bending and welding flex-resistant wire, they created filigree, truss-like structures. The visual allure of the wire pieces arises from the contrast between their lightweight appearance and high static strength.

From a formal standpoint, the Wire Chair (1951) is a 'translation' of the plastic side shell in the material of resistance-welded wire mesh. In the process of this reinterpretation, the Eameses created a chair with minimal material requirements that is also a striking synthesis of strength and transparency. To complement the biomorphically shaped shell, they designed a removable cushion which emphasises the graphic qualities of the chair. The Eameses also used bent and welded wire for the children's wardrobe Hang-It-All, designed in 1953. The wire structure, which is lacquered in white, consists of variously shaped hooks welded onto a rectangular wire frame with integrated screw attachments. The colourful wooden balls mounted on each of the hooks bring playful cheer to this practical wall sculpture.

'Why don't we make an updated version of the old English club chair?' With this comment, Charles Eames initiated the long and intricate development process of the Lounge Chair, which has become one of the Eameses' most famous designs. The original aim was to satisfy the desire for an amply proportioned, luxurious chair, while offering ultimate comfort with highest quality materials and workmanship. The Eameses set new standards with the Lounge Chair: it is not only lighter, more elegant and more modern than conventionally ponderous club chairs—it is also more comfortable.

The Eameses once described their approach to design as a 'plan for arranging elements in such a way as to best accomplish a particular purpose'. The Lounge Chair is an ideal example of this: a five-star aluminium base to bear the swivel seat construction; three separately moulded plywood shells for the seat and two-piece backrest; three thickly padded leather cushions which are snapped into the shells; leather-upholstered armrests; two steel angles, concealed by the armrests, which connect the backrest and seat; two aluminium braces to join the backrest pieces; and small parts including glides, a few screws, grommets and hooks, spacers, and four shock mounts—rubber buttons that add structural flexibility and thereby enhance the chair's comfort. In the design of the Lounge Chair, the Eameses created a successful synthesis of tradition and modernity. It is luxurious without being pretentious; it offers homey comfort without a trace of dowdiness or banality. Aluminium was the fourth and final material that the Eameses used to develop pioneering furniture designs. The chairs in the Aluminium Group, as well as other pieces derived from them, demonstrate fundamental aspects of Eames design: structural intelligence; an intimate understanding of the inherent characteristics and potential of various materials; a design approach based on industrial production methods; and the ability to perfect a basic form and then vary it for many different applications. The Aluminium Group represents the Eameses' first departure from the seat shell, which was the basis of their previous chair designs. They instead utilise the principle of tension, assigning a load-bearing function to the sling upholstery. Stretched tautly, but elastically, between the metal sides, the textile or leather sling guarantees a high degree of comfort by adapting gradually to the sitter's shape.

The Eameses were fascinated by cast aluminium because of its specific characteristics: high tensile strength, light weight, malleability and corrosion resistance. At the same time, the material posed a special challenge. Because it could be moulded into any desired shape, its form could easily become arbitrary or even whimsical—a possibility that completely contradicted the Eameses' design philosophy. The mastery with which they solved this problem is evident in the metal frame of the Aluminium Chair. In spite of its sculptural presence and slender, exceedingly elegant profile, every structural component fulfils a clearly defined, self-evident purpose, and its formal manifestation corresponds precisely to this function. So long as no other material surpasses the properties of aluminium, the structural solutions and formal appearance of the Eames Aluminium Group will remain current and exemplary—as they have for decades.

ORGANIC DESIGN COMPETITION

Year: 1940
Materials
> Structure: wood or metal
> Back and seat: a
single piece of moulded
plywood
Collaborator
Eero Saarinen

Objects presented
SIDE CHAIR (1)
EASY CHAIR (2)
RELAXATION CHAIR (3)
LOUNGING CHAIR (4)
CONVERSATION CHAIR (5)
SOFA UNIT (6)
STORAGE UNIT (7)
ORGANIC CHAIR (8)

In 1940, the director of the Museum of Modern Art (MoMA, New York) organised a competition to find new ideas in home furnishings design. Charles Eames and Eero Saarinen submitted joint pieces and won first prize in the two categories they entered. The most significant aspect of their designs in the seat furniture category was the sophisticated manufacture of a light structural shell made of plywood. The drawback became clear later, however, when attempts were made to mass-produce it at affordable prices.

In the case furniture category, they presented a low coffee table, a storage cupboard (7) and a central table. They also exhibited full-size models of some pieces of furniture.

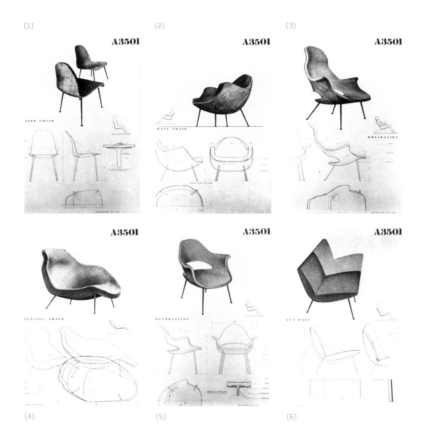

(1)

A3501

SIDE CHAIR

(2)

A3501

EASY CHAIR

(3)

A3501

RELAXATION

A3501

SEEGING SHAPE

(4)

A3501

CONVERSATION

(5)

A3501

SEA UNIT

(6)

(5)

(6)

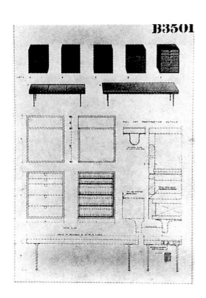

(7)

Display at the MoMA in New York of the furniture
submitted by Eero Saarinen and Charles Eames to
the Organic Design Competition (1940).

FIRST PLYWOOD PIECES

Year: 1941-1945
Materials
›Structure: plywood
(birch, mahogany or deal),
moulded using the KAZAM!
machine
Dimensions
Leg splints: 106.7 x 20.3 x
12.7 cm
Elements
Leg splints (1)
Arm splints (2)
Stretchers (3)
Plane parts (4)
Experimental chairs (5)
and sculpture (1 right)

Following the tremendous success of the pieces of furniture submitted to the MoMA competition in 1940, the Eameses began to explore the possibility of mass-producing entire high-quality, low-cost items made out of moulded and bent plywood. To do this, Charles invented a machine they called the 'KAZAM machine' (overleaf), in which a bicycle pump forced air at regular intervals of between four and six hours into an inflatable membrane in the form of a balloon. Using this machine, the piece of wood was pushed up against an electrically heated plaster mould that gave the wood the desired curve. The final finish of the piece was achieved manually using a handsaw and file.

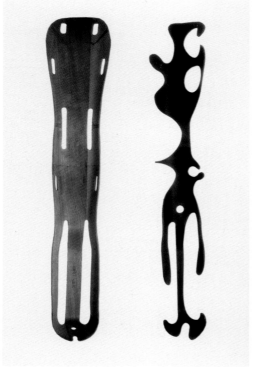

The first mass-produced objects made were leg splints for use by the military. These proved to be an excellent alternative to the metal splints then employed, as they were more flexible, lighter and adapted to the form of the human body.

(3)

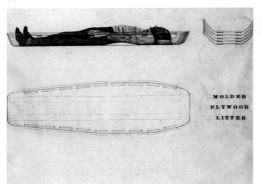

MOLDED
PLYWOOD
LITTER

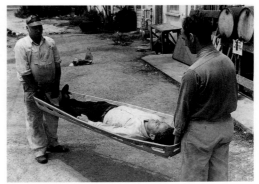

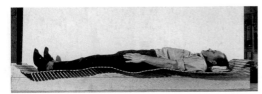

They also developed wooden plane parts for the aerospace industry to be used in place of those made of metal, which were by now in short supply due to restrictions as a result of the war. Production came to a halt after an accident in which a pilot and passenger died.

(4)

The first plywood seats had small cuts in them to
prevent them splitting and splintering.

(5)

In keeping with their determination to provide high quality at low cost, to keep their pieces simple and comfortable, and to ensure that the appearance conveyed the essence of their production method, the Eameses experimented with ways to make a single piece of wood form both the seat and back of a chair.

Five examples of their chairs with metal legs that
have an axial rocking motion.

FURNITURE AND TOYS FOR CHILDREN

Year: 1945
Materials:
›Structure: laminated and ply birch or
painted black, blue, red, magenta and yellow
Dimensions
stool: 21.6 x 38.1 x 26.7 cm
Parts
Furniture: tables, chairs and stools
Toys: elephant, horse, sea lion and frog (3), and bear (4)

The collection of furniture for children was not a market success since furniture of this type was regarded as unusual and not essential. The tables and stools were made out of a single piece of moulded wood. The chairs had a small hole the size of a child's fingers cut in the shape of a heart to make it easy to move them around.

The Eameses also made children's toys that consisted of amusing animal designs. A metal model was made of the bear, sea lion and frog toys, whereas only three models of the others were made in wood. Their toy designs were not marketed until the 1950s.

(1)

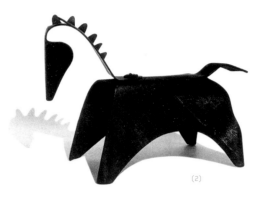

(2)

(3)

(4)

LCW & DCW

LOUNGE CHAIR WOOD & DINING CHAIR WOOD

Year: 1945-1946
Materials
›Structure: laminated
and ply rosewood, birch,
walnut and ash. Also
upholstered in fabric,
Naugahyde and leather
Dimensions
LCW (1): 67 x 56 x 56 cm
DCW (2): 74 x 43 x 53 cm
Variants
DCW with three legs

When the war ended, mass production of plywood furniture began to stabilise. The elimination of the intermediate wooden pieces required to assemble the seat and back made it possible to manufacture improved models such as the LCW (Lounge Chair Wood) (1) and DCW (Dining Chair Wood) (2). The composite models were cheaper since there was no need to rebuild the entire chair if one part broke. Initially, these models had rubber shock mounts fixed to the wood by means of a special adhesive, heat and pressure, giving the chair greater flexibility and movement. The pieces of wood did not need to be drilled to fit screws and so were left intact.

View of one of the rooms in the MoMA exhibition
"New Furniture Designed by Charles Eames"
(1946). A panel of steel cables gives the
impression of a mirrored wall. (3)

(1)

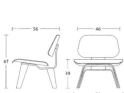

(2)

(2)

Information leaflet on the plywood furniture
designed by the Eames Office.

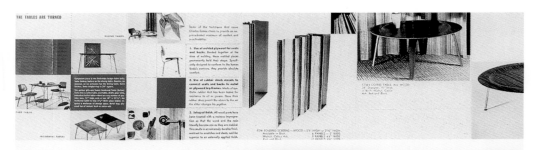

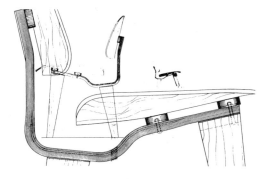

DCM & LCM

DINING CHAIR METAL & LOUNGE CHAIR METAL

Year: 1945-1946
Materials
> Structure: metal legs
> Back and seat: laminated
and ply rosewood, birch,
walnut and ash
Dimensions
DCM (1): 74 x 52 x 54 cm
LCM (2): 66 x 56 x 62 cm
Variants
DCM with three legs (3)

Following on from the DCW and LCW models, a substructure made of metal bars
was developed to form the chair legs and
central spine, thereby giving rise to two
further models, the DCM (Dining Chair
Metal) (1) and the LCM (Lounge Chair
Metal) (2). They also created an improved
model with just three legs (3), which was
regarded as having greater sales
potential, though it was later replaced by
a four-leg model after stability problems
were detected.

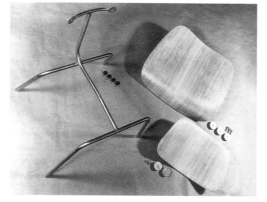

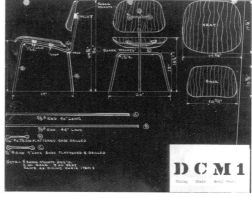

Ink on paper sketch by Ray Eames,
late 1940s.

(3)

DTW

DINING TABLE WOOD

Year: 1945-1946
Materials
>Structure:
birch plywood
Dimensions
71.1 x 137.2 x 86.4 cm
Variants
Side table (1)

The rectangular DTW (Dining Table Wood) is one of the most austere plywood tables made by the Eames Office.

They also designed a variant, a lower coffee table with square top. The legs on both tables, which are bent at a right or angle, can be removed.

SIDE TABLE

Year: 1945-1946
Materials
›Structure: metal,
lacquered in black
›Top: plywood
Dimensions
58.1 x 88.9 x 47 cm

This side table prototype came about in response to the idea of working with a structure consisting of three metal rods linked by another rod as a crosspiece. This structure would then support a rectangular wooden top with sides bent upwards in the manner of a tray. The key issue was to successfully resolve the functional and aesthetic problems involved in joining the metal elements to the wood.

CTW & CTM

COFFEE TABLE WOOD & COFFEE TABLE METAL

Year: 1945-1946
Materials
›Structure: wood or
chrome-finish metal
›Top: wood
Dimensions
40 x 86 cm (diameter)
Variants
CTW with four legs (1)
CTM with four legs

In 1945, the Plywood Division employed the wood treatment process to begin to produce table components. The first models only had three legs, but a year later, in order to begin marketing and sales, modifications were made, resulting in more stable models with four legs and self-levelling mechanisms.

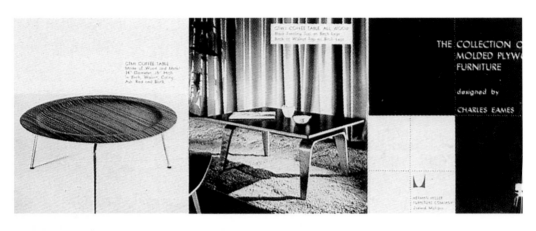

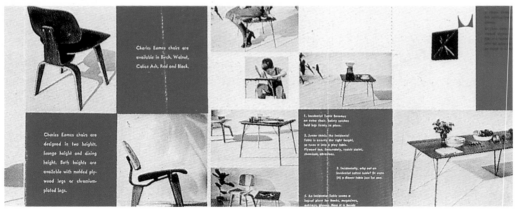

These tables were named after the material used
in the structure: CTW (Coffee Table Wood) (1)
and CTM (Coffee Table Metal). (2)

(1)

(2)

View of the living room in the Case Study House
no. 9, designed for John Entenza, in Pacific
Palisades, California (overleaf).
Exhibition at the Barclay Hotel in New York,
sponsored by Evans Products.

FSW

FOLDING WALL SCREEN

Year: 1946
Materials
plywood
Dimensions
173 x 86.5 cm (made out
of various sections,
each 24 cm wide)

Another of the experiments in plywood by the Eameses influenced by the earlier works of Alvar Aalto was their invention of a folding screen wall (FSW), made up of U-shaped modules linked together by means of flexible vinyl tapes. The final piece could be moved with relative ease and could be assembled in a wide range of different ways depending on how the modules were put together. Later models had more sophisticated and durable hinging mechanisms.

(1)

Full-page advertisement in a magazine
for Herman Miller that won a
New York Art Directors Club prize. (1)

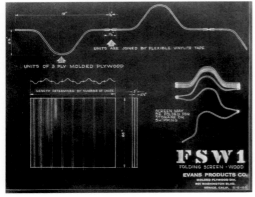

CASE GOODS

Year: 1946
Materials
plywood storage modules
with wooden exterior panels
treated in a range of ways
to provide rigidity (note the
circular reliefs)
Dimensions
various standard modules (1)

In 1945, the Eameses and Evans Products began to use their plywood technology to produce modular storage systems. The Case Goods system was based on the units that Eero Saarinen and Charles Eames had made in 1940 for the Organic Design Competition and consists of a number of wooden boxes grouped together on low benches of differing lengths. These boxes or units were available in different standard sizes and in various versions: with boxes, with shelves or fitted with a radio. Similarly, it was possible to interchange the long exterior pieces, which were treated in different ways.
The versatility of this system was able to meet every customer's specific needs.

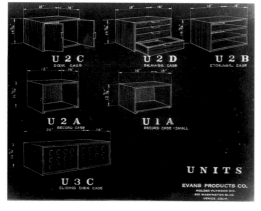

(1)

THREE FOLDING TABLES

Year: 1947
Materials
> Structure: metal
folding legs
> Top: laminated wood
Dimensions
side table:
43.2 x 54.6 x 45.7 cm

The innovative feature of these tables is the way they fold. The four legs bend and are tucked away in a hollow underneath the table top and held in place there by a metal clip. Three versions of these table were made: the square or cards table, the rectangular or dining table and the side or children's table. Even though the table was relatively easy to manufacture, a number of problems arose with the finish of the top, which had rounded edges. They experimented with the difficult process of baking a soft layer of resins on the wood to protect it from heat and dirt. The underside was covered with resin-impregnated black paper.

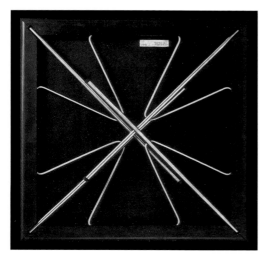

MINIMAL CHAIR

Year: 1948
Materials
> Structure: steel tubing
> Back and seat: metal mesh or solid metal

The minimal chair was an experimental seat made in keeping with the slogan "less is more" and was intended to use a minimal amount of material to achieve maximum comfort.

The Eames Office produced a prototype of this chair for the International Competition for Low-Cost Furniture Design, organised by the MoMA in 1948. Two versions were made, one with the seat and back made out of metal mesh and the other with solid metal. Despite the fact that the chair achieved a formal purity reminiscent of Cycladic sculpture, it never went into mass production.

LA CHAISE

Year: 1948
Materials
> Structure: metal rods
on an oak base
> Back and seat:
fibreglass
Dimensions
87 x 150 x 89 cm
seat height 42 cm

La Chaise is the most sculptural of all the chairs the Eameses designed. Its name is an acknowledgement of the *Floating Sculpture* (1927) by Gaston Lachaise (1). It is made out of fibreglass shaped in a single mould and rests on an unusual or metal and wooden base: a tubular steel frame supported by two pieces of oak arranged in a cross. Even though La Chaise was included in the permanent collection of the Museum of Modern Art, it was or never produced during the life of the designers and was not manufactured commercially until 1990.

Ray working on the mould for La Chaise with members
of the studio (full-size model for the MoMA competition).

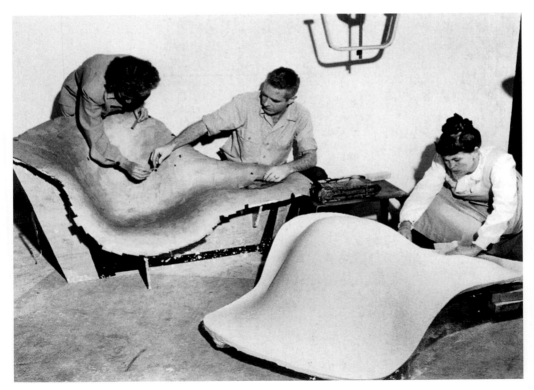

(1)

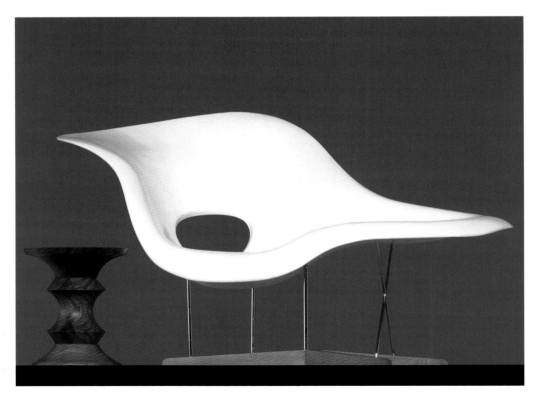

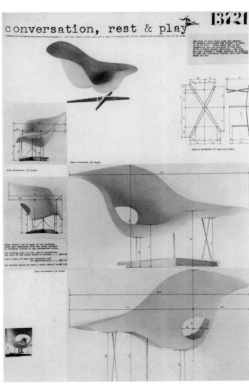

ESU

EAMES STORAGE UNITS

Year: 1950
Materials
›Structure: chrome-finish steel with bracing rods
›Components: plywood drawers and shelves finished with birch or walnut, or laminated with black plastic
›Internal panels: Masonite in eight colours
›Sliding doors: pressed wood and white fibreglass
Dimensions
100 series:
51 x 61 x 41 cm
200 series:
102 x 119 x 41 cm
400 series:
204 x 119 x 41 cm

The basic principles of the Eameses' design philosophy are evident in these innovative industrial storage units, which are characterised by the purity of their minimalist lines and their practicality, affordability and modular design. The Herman Miller showroom exhibited the furniture in a display that suggested a number of possible installations suitable for use in the home or office. The cardboard box in which the furniture was packed for distribution was also designed by the Eameses and could be turned into a toy house for children.

Drawing by Ray for the room at the
"For Modern Living" exhibition, Detroit, 1949.

Explanatory leaflet showing possible ways of
assembling the ESU system.

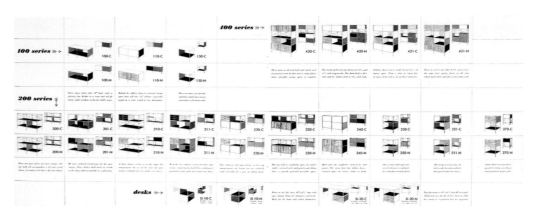

LTR & ETR

LOW TABLE ROD BASE & ELLIPTICAL TABLE ROD BASE

Year: 1950-1951
Materials:
› Structure: U-shaped metal rods with crossed ties
› Top: 19-mm-thick plywood in natural wood finish or laminated in black or white with bevelled edges
Dimensions
LTR (1): 25.4 x 39.4 x 33 cm
ETR (2): 25 x 230 x 73 cm

Low Table Rod Base (LTR) (1) was one of the innovations in the line created in 1950 and is a small occasional table made of plywood with a base consisting of two U-shaped metal rods with crossed ties to improve stability.

In 1951, the same base was used at each of the ends of the Elliptical Table Rod Base (ETR) (2). The top was laminated in black plastic. Its low height (just 25 cm) invited people to sit on the ground to use this table, which was popularly known as the Surfboard.

(1)

PLASTIC CHAIR
AND EASY CHAIR

Year: 1950-1953
Materials
› Structure: six
alternative bases:
swivel, wooden legs,
tubular metal legs, wire
rods in the manner of
the Eiffel Tower, cast
aluminium pedestal with
wheels and a rocking
chair version with birch
rockers and wire rods
› Back and seat:
polyester plastic
reinforced with
fibreglass
Dimensions
Chair: 34 x 55 x 47 cm
seat height 46 cm
Variants
Stacking chair, 1955

When the advances in plastics technology developed during the Second World War became accessible to the general populace once the war was over, the Eameses decided to use this material in their furniture. Their first fibreglass chair was made in 1948 as a prototype for the International Competition for Low-Cost Furniture Design, organised by the MoMA. Manufactured by Zenith Plastics, they were made out of the same material employed by the company in its radars and were the first commercial use of plastic for seats.

In 1950, therefore, the Eameses had achieved their goal of mass-producing furniture with curves. In the early days, the material came in the natural marbled colours of fibreglass: parchment, grey and beige. Primary colours were offered later.

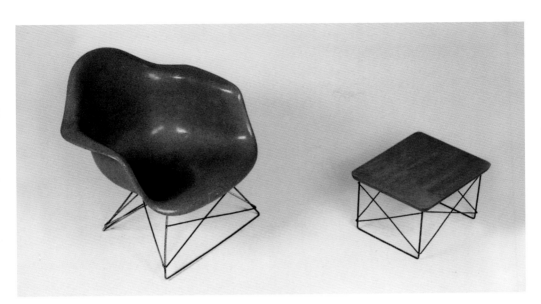

STACKING CHAIR
Year: 1955
Materials
›Structure: metal legs
›Back and seat: polyester
plastic reinforced with
fibreglass
Dimensions
34 x 55 x 47 cm
seat height 46 cm

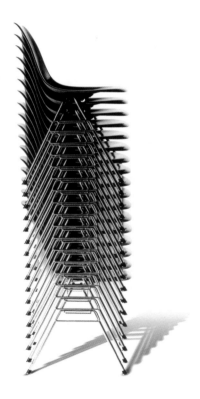

A simple system of metal hooks linked to
U-shaped legs made it easy to stack the chairs
vertically and to link them together horizontally.
These chairs were used widely in conference halls
and classrooms.

The plastic chairs and easy chairs provided the starting point for the first multiple chairs for public spaces. These chairs had structures consisting of aluminium legs with rubber feet and steel rods to secure the seats in place, and were used as seating in stadiums (Stadium Seating) in 1954 (1), as tandem seats (Tandem Shell Seating) in 1963 (2) and as school chairs with a desk-type arm (School Seating) in 1964. (3)

(2)

(1)

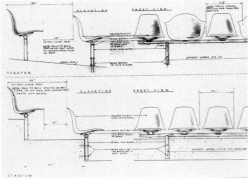

3

METAL MESH CHAIR

Year: 1951-1953
Materials
> Structure: six alternative bases: swivel, wooden legs, tubular metal legs, wire rods in the manner of the Eiffel Tower, cast aluminium pedestal with wheels and a rocking chair version with birch rockers and wire rods
> Seat and back: a single piece of metal mesh, folded and welded
Option of full or partial upholstery with padding that formed triangular cushioning in the seat and on the back (Bikini model) (1)
> Upholstery materials: black or brown leather, vinyl, cinnamon-coloured cotton, tweed hessian and fabric with a harlequin pattern
Dimensions
84 x 49 x 53 cm

The Metal Mesh Chair is another example of the adaptation of industrial technology to furniture manufacturing. It was designed as a plastic chair with stacking base units. The Eames Office's knowledge of resistance welding of metal rods was also necessary in the creation of this chair. The mesh was more densely woven at the centre to make it more rigid and had open horizontal lines at the sides. The chair surround was made of a doubled length of wire of thicker gauge to give it greater stability. The distance between the structural units meant that this chair was lighter than other mesh chairs being manufactured at that time.

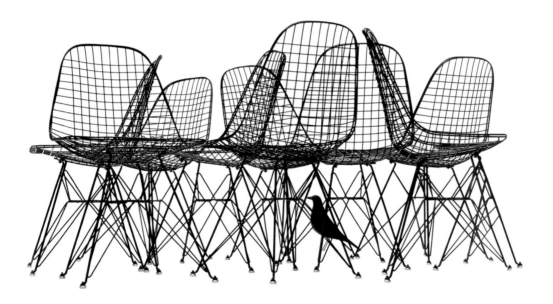

One of the first welding moulds for prototype
bases. (2)

(2)

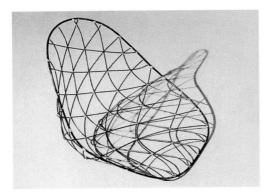
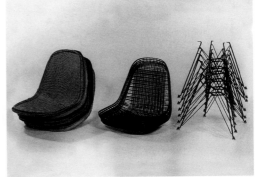

METAL MESH SOFA

Year: 1951
Materials:
›Structure: four
cable trusses on long
wooden feet
›Seat and back: metal
mesh with upholstery
consisting of three
cushions joined together

The Metal Mesh Sofa was made using the same materials and technology as the Metal Mesh Chair. It was designed as a sofa that could be easily assembled and moved by the customer, as its high back could be folded down. It was light in weight and appearance and was intended to be a cheap item of furniture. Even though it was innovative and made out of industrial materials, it was never mass-produced, as just two prototypes in two different sizes were made. Even so, the basic concept and form were later used in the Sofa Compact.

The mesh sofa in the living room
of Kwikset House (1951).

TOYS

Year: The Toy (1951),
The Little Toy (1952),
House of Cards (1952),
House of Cards Giant
(1953)
Variant
Picture Deck (1)

The Eameses designed toys as part of their research while working on their furnishings, films and other projects. The Toy was a construction game intended for children and adults alike to play inside. Brightly coloured geometrical or panels were linked using wooden rods to create infinite three-dimensional forms. The Little Toy was a variant on a smaller scale. One of their most surprising, innovative and commercially successful products was their House of Cards (1), which consisted of a set of 54 cards with illustrations on one side and six slits cut into them, one at each end and two along each of the sides. These slits enabled the cards to be assembled into countless architectural variations. Ray was responsible for selecting the images. The House of Cards Giant (2) consisted of 20 cards measuring 18 x 27 cm.

Ray with a prototype of The Toy, made out of cardboard triangles. The Eameses later added square sections, which made it easier to build taller constructions.

HANG-IT-ALL

Year: 1953
Materials
> Structure: metal rods
and painted wooden
balls
Dimensions
35.6 x 50.8 x 14 cm

Hang-It-All is a rack with hooks designed for children to use to hang all kinds of belongings from, such as a toy or coat. A mass-production system was used to weld a number of metal rods simultaneously, the same system that inspired the wire chair and LTR table.

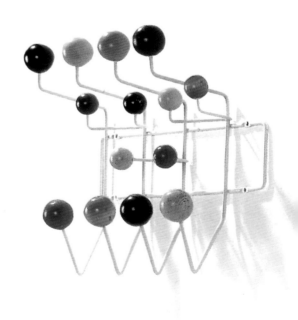

SOFA COMPACT

Year: 1954
Materials
> Structure: square-sectioned, chrome-finish, steel legs and black enamelled steel frame
> Back and seat: three urethane foam cushions joined together and upholstered in leather
Dimensions
89 x 185 x 54 cm

The Sofa Compact was the last piece of furniture that the Eames designed with the intention that it should be low cost. It was also the first mass-produced sofa design. It is based on the Eames House chair (1949) and uses ideas developed in 1951 for the Metal Mesh Sofa. This sofa is the least sculptural of the Eameses' metal pieces of furniture, since its back was designed in such a way as to ensure that it could be folded in order to make it easier to transport and store.

(1)

Herman Miller photograph to advertise
the Sofa Compact, taken in a dentist's
waiting room. (1)

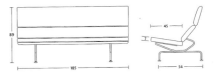

LOUNGE CHAIR AND OTTOMAN

Year: 1956
Materials
> Structure: three
curving pieces of
rosewood plywood
for the seat and one
piece of the same
characteristics for
the footstool
> Base: swivel, five-
pointed star mechanism
with five cast aluminium
feet finished in matt black
> Back and seat:
upholstered in black
leather with buttons and
filled with foam, down
and duck feathers
Dimensions
chair 80 x 83 x 89 cm
footstool 43 x 60 x 64 cm

The history of the Lounge chair dates back to the easy chair that Charles and Eero Saarinen showed in the MoMA "Organic Design in Home Furnishings" exhibition in 1940. In 1945-1946, the Eameses worked on and experimented with a chair made out of three pieces of plywood that came close to what they were hoping to achieve. They gave the first model as a gift to their friend the film director Billy Wilder. Charles wanted it to have the warm and welcoming look of a well-used baseball glove.

Charles and Ray in the living room of their home:
Case Study House no. 8 (1945-1949).

Explanatory drawing of all the component parts of the
Lounge Chair and Ottoman by Charles Kratka, with
calligraphy by Sister Corita Kent of the Immaculate
Heart College. (1)

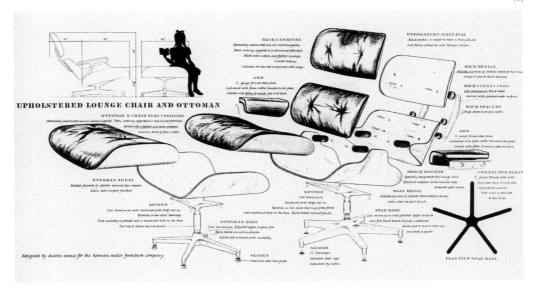

SOLAR MACHINE

Year: 1957
Materials
›Structure: aluminium

In 1957, Alcoa (the Aluminium Company of America) invited Charles and other designers to create new aluminium products to promote the use of this metal. They designed a toy, the Solar Do-Nothing Machine that used photovoltaic cells to explore the combined potential of aluminium and solar energy.

ALUMINIUM GROUP

Year: 1958-1969
Materials
›Structure: aluminium
rods on a swivel base
›Back and seat: a long
length of reversible
Naugahyde upholstery
with nylon and vinyl
foam filling
Dimensions
Variable
Co-designer
Alexander Girard
Elements
chairs with high and low
back, with or without
arms, footstool, dining
table with matching
chairs
Variants
Soft Pad Group (1969)

The aluminium collection was first mooted when Alexander Girard needed to create a line of furniture for Irwin Miller House in Columbus, Colorado, a project that he was designing in collaboration with Eero Saarinen. He was looking for furnishings that were light enough in weight to be carried outside and which would also be able to withstand the corrosive effects of the weather. Girard and the Eames team produced an elegant and minimalist design. In 1969, they created the Soft Pad Group, a derivation of the aluminium furniture with different seats and backs, covered in this case by rectangular cush-ions and padding.

SOFT PAD GROUP
Year: 1969
Materials
›Structure: aluminium
bars on a swivel base
›Back and seat: 5-cm
thick foam cushions
covered
in cotton fibre
Finished in leather
Dimensions
Variable
Elements
SIDE CHAIR
MANAGEMENT CHAIR
EXECUTIVE CHAIR
LOUNGE CHAIR (1) AND
OTTOMAN

(1)

EA 222

EA 217   EA 205, 206   EA 223

CHAISE

Year: 1968
Materials
›Structure: aluminium
bars
›Seat: six foam cushions
covered in black leather
Dimensions
71.1 x 200.7 x 44.5 cm

This item of furniture was designed especially for the film director Billy Wilder, a friend of the Eameses. The narrow width of the seat, at just 44.5 cm, was specifically requested by Wilder and gives the piece its highly stylised lines, which are further emphasised by the simplicity of the two legs, made of a single piece of aluminium, that form the main structural frame.

The Chaise was manufactured by Herman Miller in 1968 and remains in production today, now made of aluminium sheathed in aubergine-coloured nylon.

LOBBY CHAIR AND STOOL

Year: 1960
Materials
Lobby Chair:
›Structure:
aluminium bars
›Back and seat:
upholstered in leather
›Stool: walnut
Dimensions
›Lobby Chair:
86-92 x 74 x 68 cm
›Stool:
38 x 33 cm (diameter)

In 1960, the Eames Office was commissioned to design three waiting and rest rooms in the Time & Life Building in the Rockefeller Center in New York. They designed the flooring, lighting, walls and items of furniture, among them a chair. This chair had to be smaller in size than the Lounge Chair and was also expected to serve as a conference hall chair. Ray designed four wooden stools, all very similar but with different central sections, that went with the chairs as low tables or as seats. A year later, Herman Miller introduced the Eames Executive Desk Chair, a modified version of the Time-Life Chair in that it was narrower and had an adjustable and movable back, making it suitable as an office chair.

ECS

EAMES CONTRACT STORAGE

Year: 1961
Materials
›Structure: aluminium,
wood partitions, black
phenolic plastic to
protect the edges

These units, consisting of three cup-
boards, a work station and a bed, were
designed as a reflection on the furniture requirements of a bedroom in a hall
of residence. The units were raised off
the floor and did not extend as far as the
ceiling, thereby leaving the modules open
at the top and the bottom and so ensuring
that they were constantly aired.

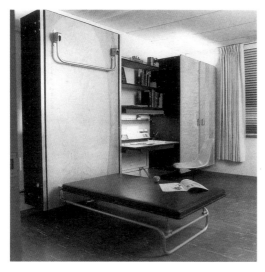

TANDEM SLING SEATING

Year: 1962
Materials
> Structure: aluminium
> Back and seat: sheets
of black or coloured
Naugahyde filled with
vinyl and nylon foam
Collaborator
C. F. Murphy

The Eameses were commissioned to design the Tandem system by Eero Saarinen Associates and C. F. Murphy Associates, who were looking for a multiple seating system for the airports they were designing (Dulles, Washington, and O'Hare, Chicago, respectively). The system consisted of a group of two to ten seats side by side or back to back. In structure, they were reminiscent of the Aluminium Group, while the back and seat were formed by separate, interchangeable parts. The material had to be hardwearing and long-lasting and hence was subjected to strict quality controls.

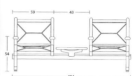

CHRONOLOGY

STORAGE UNIT
1940
pp. 18-23

CONVERSATION
CHAIR 1940
pp. 18-23

EASY CHAIR
1940
pp. 18-23

COFFEE TABLE
1940
pp. 18-23

LOUNGING CHAIR
1940
pp. 18-23

RELAXATION CHAIR
1940
pp. 18-23

SIDE CHAIR
1940
pp. 18-23

SOFA UNIT
1940
pp. 18-23

SEATS AND BACKS
1941-1945
pp. 24-33

SCULPTURES
1941-1945

PLANE PARTS
1941-1945
pp. 24-33

ARM SPLINTS
1941-1945
pp. 24-33

LEG SPLINT AND
SCULTURE
1941-1945
pp. 24-33

COVER FOR *ARTS &
ARCHITECTURE*
1942-1947

EXPERIMENTAL CHAIR
1945
pp. 24-33

EXPERIMENTAL
ROCKING CHAIR 1945
pp. 24-30

TOY ANIMALS
1945
pp. 34-37

CHILDREN'S FURNITURE
1945
pp. 34-37

LCW
1945-1946
pp. 38-41

DCW
1945-1946
pp. 38-41

DCW
WITH THREE LEGS
1945-1946

DCM
1945-1946
pp. 42-45

LCM
1945-1946
pp. 42-45

DCM WITH THREE LEGS
1945-1946
pp. 42-45

DTW
1945-1946
pp. 46-47

SIDE TABLE
1945-1946
pp. 48-49

CTM FOUR LEGS
1945-1946
pp. 50-54

CTM THREE LEGS
1945-1946
pp. 50-54

CTW FOUR LEGS
1945-1946
pp. 50-54

CTW THREE LEGS
1945-1946
p. 52

FOLDING TABLE
1945-1946

FSW
1946
pp. 54-55

RADIO HOUSING
1946

CASE GOODS
1946
pp. 56-57

FOLDING TABLES
1947
pp. 58-59

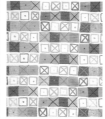

TELA CROSSPATCH
1947

MINIMAL CHAIR
1948
pp. 60-61

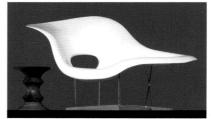

LA CHAISE
1948
pp. 62-67

ESU
1950
pp. 68-71

MASK
1950

LTR
1950
pp. 72-75

ETR
1950
pp. 72-75

PLASTIC ARMCHAIR
1950-1953
pp. 76-83

PLASTIC CHAIR
1950-1953
pp. 76-83

WIRE SOFA
1951
pp. 88-91

THE TOY
1951-1953
pp. 92-95

**METAL MESH EASY
CHAIR**
1951-1953

METAL MESH CHAIR
1951-1953
pp. 84-87

HOUSE OF CARDS
1952
pp. 92-95

THE LITTLE TOY
1952
pp. 92-95

HOUSE OF CARDS GIANT
1953
pp. 92-95

HANG-IT-ALL
1953
pp. 96-97

SOFA COMPACT
1954
pp. 98-99

**COMPACT
CUPBOARD**
1954

STACKING CHAIR
1955

COLOURING-IN
1956

LOUNGE CHAIR AND OTTOMAN
1956
pp. 100-103

**STEPHENS
LOUDSPEAKER**
1956

SOLAR MACHINE
1957
pp. 104-105

ALUMINIUM GROUP
SIDE CHAIR 1958
pp. 106-111

ALUMINIUM GROUP
SIDE CHAIR 1958
pp. 106-111

ALUMINIUM GROUP LOUNGE CHAIR AND
OTTOMAN 1958
pp. 106-111

REVELL TOY HOUSE
1959

LOBBY CHAIR
1960
pp. 112-113

EXECUTIVE DESK
CHAIR
1960

STOOLS
1960
pp. 112-113

LA FONDA EASY CHAIR
1961

ECS
1961
pp. 114-115

LA FONDA TABLE
1961

TANDEM SLING
SEATING 1962
pp. 116-117

SEGMENTED BASE TABLE
1964

SOFA
1964

INTERMEDIATE
DESK CHAIR
1968

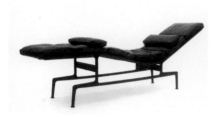

SOFT PAD CHAISE
1968
pp. 110-111

SOFT PAD LOUNGE
CHAIR
1969

SOFT PAD MANAGE-
MENT CHAIR
1969

DRAFTING CHAIR
1970

BUT-SOFA LOOSE CUSHION
1971

NEWTON HOUSE OF CARDS
1974

SOFA
1984

BIBLIOGRAPHY

Baroni, Daniele: "La forma e il suo doppio: L'immagine e la metodologia del proggeto". *Ottagono*, [June 1981], Milan, pp. 78-85.

Capplan, Ralph: *By design*. St. Martin's Press, New York, 1982.

The Design of Herman Miller: Pionereed by Eames, Girard, Nelson, Propst, Rohde. Whitney Library of Design, New York, 1976.

"Experiencing Eames" in *ID* [January-February 1990], New York, pp. 62-69.

Drexler, Arthur: *Charles Eames: Furniture from the Design Collection*. The Museum of Modern Art, New York, 1973.

Eames, Charles: "A Prediction: less self-expression for the designer " in *Print*, [January-Februay 1960], New York, pp. 77-79.

"Design, designer and industry" in *Magazine of Art* [December 1951], New York, pp. 320-321.

"Organic design": *California Arts & Architecture*, [December 1941], San Francisco, pp. 16-17.

Eames, Charles and Ray: *"Eames report"* (Also known as *"India report"*), Eames Office, Los Angeles, 1958.

Eames, Charles and Ray. *Re-connections: the work of the Eames Office*. New Haven: Yale University School of Architecture, 1999.

Eames, Demetrios. *Eames: beautiful details*, Gloria Fowler, Steve Crist (eds.). Los Angeles: AMMO Books, 2012.

Eidelberg, Martin et al: *The Eames lounge chair: an icon of modern design*. Merrell, London, 2006.

Friedman, Mildred S.: *Nelson / Eames / Girard / Propst: The design process at Herman Miller*. Design Quarterly, Vancouver, 1999.

Herman Miller Inc: *The Herman Miller Collection 1952: Furniture designed by George Nelson and Charles Eames, with occasional pieces by Isamu Noguchi, Peter Hvidt, and O. M. Nielson*, Acanthus Press, New York, 1995.

Ince, Catherine; Johnson, Lotte (eds.). *The World of Charles and Ray Eames*. London: Thames & Hudson Ltd, 2018.

Kirkham, Pat: *Charles and Ray Eames: Designers of the Twentieth Century*. The MIT Press, Cambridge, Massachusets, 1995.

Koening, Gloria. *Eames*. Tachen, Colonia, 2007.

Kugler, Jolanthe. *Eames Furniture Sourcebook*. Weil am Rhein: Germany Vitra Design Museum 2017.

Neuhart, John; Neuhart,Marilyn: *Connections: the work of Charles and Ray Eames*, UCLA Art Council, Los Angeles, 1976.

Eames House, Ernst & Sohn and Academy Editions, Berlin and London, 1994.

Organic design in home furnishings. The Museum of Modern Art, New York, 1941.

Neuhart, John; Neuhart; Marilyn Eames; Ray: *Eames design: The work of the office of Charles and Ray Eames*. Abrams, New York, 1989.

Ostroff, Daniel (ed). *An Eames Anthology: Articles, Film Scripts, Interviews, Letters, Notes, Speeches by Charles and Ray Eames*. New Haven: Yale University Press, 2015.

Prouvé, Jean. *Charles & Ray Eames. Die großen Konstrukteure – Parallelen und Unterschiede*. Weil am Rhein: Vitra Design Museum, 2002.

Quinton, Maryse. *Charles & Ray Eames*. Paris: Éditions de la Martinière, 2015.

Rubino, Luciano: *Ray & Charles Eames. Il collettivo della fantasia*. Edizioni Kappa, Rome, 1981.

Smithson, Peter, and Smithson, Alison: "Eames celebration" in *Architectural design* [September 1996] special issue, New York, pp. 432-71.

Stungo, Naomi: *Charles and Ray Eames*, Carlton Books, London, 2002.